The Way Through the Wilderness

by
Roy Porter

Grosvenor House
Publishing Limited

All rights reserved
Copyright © **Roy Porter**, 2016

The right of **Roy Porter** to be identified as the author of this
work has been asserted in accordance with Section 78
of the Copyright, Designs and Patents Act 1988

The book cover picture is copyright to Artisteer

This book is published by
Grosvenor House Publishing Ltd
Link House
140 The Broadway, Tolworth, Surrey, Kt6 7Ht.
www.grosvenorhousepublishing.co.uk

This book is sold subject to the conditions that it shall not, by way of
trade or otherwise, be lent, resold, hired out or otherwise circulated
without the author's or publisher's prior consent in any form of binding or
cover other than that in which it is published and
without a similar condition including this condition being imposed
on the subsequent purchaser.

A CIP record for this book
is available from the British Library

ISBN **978-1-78623-792-7**

'All Scripture quotations are taken from the
New International Version of the Bible unless otherwise noted.'

Contents

1. 'Lord, please make my brown eyes blue.'   1
2. Hupernikaó   4
3. Overcoming the past   6
4. 'Eloi, Eloi, Lema Sabacthani' (Mark 15:34)   8
5. In the Beginning God   10
6. The Greatest Verse in the Bible   12
7. 'Intimacy with God'   13
8. My Friend Mrs P.   15
9. Mountains and Valleys   17
10. Reflections   20
11. Encouragement 1   22
12. Encouragement 2   24
13. Encouragement 3   26
14. Encouragement 4   29
15. Encouragement 5   32
16. Encouragement 6   34
17. Spiritual Health   37

Contents

18.	You are God's child	40
19.	Dealing with Doubt	42
20.	Marching On!	45
21.	The New Life	48
22.	Victorious Living (1)	50
23.	Victorious Living (2)	53
24.	Blessed Assurance	55
25.	Will You Go?	57
26.	Ransomed *healed, restored, forgiven*	59
27.	*ransomed* Healed *restored, forgiven*	61
28.	*ransomed, healed,* Restored, *forgiven*	64
29.	*ransomed, healed, restored,* Forgiven	66
30.	Vedi, Veni, Veci	69
31a.	Nevertheless	71
31b.	The Dream	74

1.

'Lord, please make my brown eyes blue.'

Amy Carmichael was the lass from Northern Ireland who wanted God to make her brown eyes blue. During our ministry with Child Evangelism Fellowship®, Anne and Karen loved teaching the story of Amy Carmichael in the various Bible clubs held in Northern Ireland and on the Isle of Man. The story tells how because she had brown eyes, she could colour her skin, dress in Indian clothes and go into temples, from which she could rescue children. Great story and well worth reading.

But recently I read her article 'Thy Brother's Blood Crieth' in which she tells of her vision. Her vision was of a great chasm and hundreds of people, men, women and children, mothers carrying babies, rushing blindly towards it. Then she saw people frantically trying to position guards at intervals to try and halt the onrush, but the gaps between the guards were too wide. Then she noticed groups of people sitting on the

'Lord, please make my brown eyes blue.'

grass with their backs toward the chasm. They were busy making daisy chains. Occasionally the cries of the dying disturbed them but even those who would rise to help were discouraged with, 'Why should you get all excited about it? Wait for a definite call to go. Anyway, you haven't finished making your daisy chain.'

Amy was among ignorant savages when this vision occurred but even in this spiritually enlightened society there are still countless numbers of people, young and old, rushing towards their chasm: an eternity without God, without salvation. Some do so blindly; some with an 'I don't really believe God would let me fall over.' Attitude, forgetting that, speaking of Jesus, Peter states,

'Salvation is found in no one else, for there is no other name under heaven given to mankind by which we must be saved.' (Acts 4:12).

There are so many with a 'couldn't care less' attitude, and still those who believe they should turn away but somehow the lure persists. There are so many other reasons why the onrush continues and, as in Amy's vision, the gap between the guards is still too wide.

When promoting the vision of Child Evangelism Fellowship®, workers would use the slogan: PRAY, GIVE, GO! with regards to the spreading of the gospel. – I believe there are many reading this who:
PRAY – Hallelujah! And I also believe that there are many reading this who:
GIVE – Another hallelujah! – But, and referring back to Amy's vision, it is the overwhelming desire of this writer to see more people prepared to:

'Lord, please make my brown eyes blue.'

GO! – We read in Matthew 9:36–38 that: 'He (Jesus) looked at the crowds and He had compassion on them, because they were harassed and helpless, like sheep without a shepherd.'

Then he said to His disciples, 'The harvest is plentiful but the workers are few. Ask the Lord of the harvest, therefore, to send out workers into his harvest field.'

2.

Hupernikaó

As I thought of Easter as the season of victory, thanks be to our Lord Jesus, I was led to consider again this wonderful portion from Paul's letter to the Romans.

In Romans 8:37–39 New King James Version we read:
'Yet in all these things we are more than conquerors through Him who loved us. For I am persuaded that neither death nor life, nor angels nor principalities nor powers, nor things present nor things to come, nor height nor depth, nor any other created thing, shall be able to separate us from the love of God which is in Christ Jesus our Lord.'

This, I believe, is the only place in Scripture where the Greek term hupernikaó is used meaning to be more than a conqueror.

I've known many conquerors in the secular world. One, in particular, is the late great boxer Rocky Marciano, known

Hupernikaó

as the Brockton Blockbuster, forty-nine fights; retired undefeated!

The Bible too has conquerors. David over Goliath, Samson over the Philistines, great men. BUT, if you are in Christ, saved by grace through faith, then YOU are greater than Rocky, greater even than David or Samson. How do I know? Because the Bible tells me so – hupernikaó, to be more than a conqueror. And this is me! I know for certain because I am trusting in the greatest Conqueror of all; he conquered temptation, he conquered death, he conquered the grave, he conquered time and space. He is Jesus Christ, King of kings and Lord of all. And he has empowered me to rise when I fall, overcome when I am tempted, walk with him and live with him in the power of his Spirit. Praise be to our God that by the work accomplished by our Saviour we, who are his conquerors, have the blessed assurance of victory in this life and joy and glory to come in the life ever after.

3.

Overcoming the past

We've all had them I'm sure; 'embarrassing moments'. I was reminded of one such moment recently. Anne and I had attended the wedding of two young friends and at the reception I was asked to say a few words having known this couple for some years. What the gathered guests didn't know, however, was that just before this I had had an accident with a zip which got stuck and refused to close. The zip was in the trousers, say no more. So I carefully made my way around my chair and made my speech from there. I did explain to the bride and groom why I had done this but I have obviously not lived the incident down. There have been other embarrassing moments but these will remain secret.

Christians are also reminded of, not just embarrassing moments we wish could go away, but also of past mistakes which dog our memories. I tell you, Satan just loves to drag up the unfortunate past especially where sin is involved. That is why we Christians should cling with hope and assurance to

Overcoming the past

verses like: 'Therefore, if anyone is in Christ, he is a new creation; the old has gone, the new has come!' (2 Corinthians 5:17–19). All this is from God, who reconciled us to himself through Christ and gave us the ministry of reconciliation: that God was reconciling the world to himself in Christ, not counting men's sins against them. And he has committed to us the message of reconciliation.' Or others such as:

'I, even I, am he who blots out
your transgressions, for my own sake,
and remembers your sins no more.' (Isaiah 43:2).
And,
'. . . for I will forgive their wickedness
and will remember their sins no more.' (Jeremiah 31:34).
As Christians, however, we still have to accept the consequences of all our past sinful – and perhaps hurtful – thoughts, words, and deeds. But God's Word refreshingly reminds that:
'If we confess our sins, he is faithful and just and will forgive us our sins and purify us from all unrighteousness.' (1 John 1:9)

Do not heed the enemy. Satan will use all his wiles to bring you discomfort and discouragement. So, place everything before the Saviour and accept his peace. As Paul reminds us in his letter to the Colossians:
'And through him to reconcile to himself all things, whether things on earth or things in heaven, by making peace through his blood, shed on the cross.'(Colossians 1:20)

4.

'Eloi, Eloi, Lema Sabacthani' (Mark 15:34)

Once again, as we look at the cross and hear the agonising cry of Jesus, his cry reminds and hopefully challenges us about the **HELL** from which we have been rescued or from which it is important to run. Jesus suffered **separation from the Father** who once said, 'This is my Son, whom I love; with him I am well pleased.' (Matthew 3:17). During this time Jesus experienced what **hell** truly is, so that no one needs to go there if he or she has trusted him as the saviour who paid sins ransom. Imagine the scene. For three hours Jesus and those crucified with him, hung in darkness.

'It was now about noon, and darkness came over the whole land until three in the afternoon, for the sun stopped shining. And the curtain of the temple was torn in two. Jesus called out with a loud voice, 'Father, into your hands I commit my spirit.' When he had said this, he breathed his last.' (Luke 23:44–46)

'Eloi, Eloi, Lema Sabacthani' (Mark 15:34)

The cross also reminds us of the **LOVE** God showed in Jesus. As Paul states, 'But God demonstrates his own love in this: While we were still sinners, Christ died for us.' (Romans 5:8).

> 'Oh the love that drew salvation so plan.
> Oh the grace that brought it down to man.
> Oh the mighty gulf that God did span at Calvary!
> Mercy there was great, and grace was free;
> There my burdened soul found liberty at Calvary
> (William R. Newell)

At the cross we see also **HOPE**. As Jesus breathed his last, the thick temple curtain was torn in two opening up the way into the holy of holies. His signifies to the world today that the path to God and his love and forgiveness, is open to all who will come to him through Christ. There is no barrier of good works or penance, which can never bring salvation, but by repentance (the turning away from sin to God) and faith (in the finished work of Christ), the barriers are gone and salvation is available for all to receive.

'Salvation is found in no one else, for there is no other name under heaven given to mankind by which we must be saved.' (Acts 4:12).

5.

In the Beginning God

As I lay in bed in a clinic in Cyprus recovering from my heart attack, the above four words kept going around and around in my head. As the days passed I began to reflect more and more on these words and especially on my great creator God. I began to think that, like myself, perhaps we as Christians fail to realize how amazing our God is: and also, how big is the gap that can exist between us and our God. From our side this gap is unbridgeable and if this gap is to be bridged it must be from God's side – for God is holy. To be holy means 'to be set apart.' God is totally separated from sin; from its power, its practice and its presence. He is absolute righteousness so, if we are to approach God we must do so on God's terms. We must be holy for, as scripture says:

'Be holy because I, the LORD your God, am holy.' (Lev. 19:2 1 Peter 1:16)

In the Beginning God

Reader, mark this – any holiness which falls short of God's holiness will not be acceptable in God's presence. This became very clear as Anne and I watched 'The Secret' on television (the story of a Christian couple who gave into temptation). It brought again to mind that Bible verse: 'Therefore let anyone who thinks that he stands take heed lest he fall.' (1st Corinthians 10:12: ESV). To stand, therefore, acceptable in the presence of God, we must have the holiness that can only come through New Life in Christ. And how is this new life found? By obedience to the **total** message of the Gospel.

6.

The Greatest verse in the Bible.

Or as some call it: 'The Gospel in a nutshell'

Thoughts from this most famous of verses:

John 3:16 (NKJV)

'God' – The greatest person

'so loved' – the greatest devotion

'the world' – the greatest number

'He gave' – the greatest act

'His only begotten Son' – the greatest gift

'that whoever believes' – the greatest condition

'should not perish' – the greatest mercy

'have everlasting life' – the greatest result

7.

'Intimacy with God'

As I read through Psalm 42 yesterday, I asked myself, 'Is the greatest desire in my life for God alone?' I realised that the answer is no, but should be. Perhaps, like myself you are not 'panting' after the material things of this world but you desire to be, in worldly terms, comfortable. Although I have absolute assurance of my salvation and God's word assures me in Romans 8:38 & 39: 'For I am convinced that neither death nor life, neither angels nor demons, neither the present nor the future, nor any powers, neither height nor depth, nor anything else in all creation, will be able to separate us from the love of God that is in Christ Jesus our Lord.'

The old sinful nature still struggles to gain control. I admit that I sometimes spiritually wilt under the struggle, so it was gratifying to read the instruction of verse 11 of the psalm. 'Why, my soul, are you downcast? Why so disturbed within me? Put your hope in God, for I will yet praise him, my

'Intimacy with God'

Saviour and my God'. As I read the psalm, I also found myself singing once again with Ian White, a Scottish singer-songwriter, and friend, whose musical interpretations of the psalms Anne and I have enjoyed for many years. So, perhaps you too are 'wilting' as you struggle to keep your spiritual focus on God, put your hope in God, rejoice in praising Him who is your rock, your saviour, and your overcoming God.

8.

My Friend Mrs P.

I have had the privilege of speaking at the funerals of Christians, and I call it a privilege because I had personally known those who have gone before. I would like to share each of what I call their spiritual conditions, but space permits only one example.

Anne and I met Mrs P when she was first of all –
Without Christ: Mrs P was not a bad person. She had been a Church organist, had played piano at gospel meetings; indeed, she had heard many gospel messages. Mrs P knew what it was to be a Christian, but had never committed her life to Jesus. She was without Christ at this stage of her life. But, praise God, He wasn't finished with her life. It was with great joy that I came to know Mrs P –
In Christ: Her conversion happened in a most peculiar way. Mrs. P was quite elderly and not too good on her feet. The bungalow in which she lived had a steep driveway and steps leading up to the door. On one occasion, on a very blowy day,

as she mounted the steps, the wind caught her and she went tumbling part way down the drive. As she lay there unable to move the thought suddenly came to her that if she were to die on this driveway she would not go to heaven. The Holy Spirit was obviously speaking to Mrs P so, there and then, she made her commitment to Christ. Not only did she receive forgiveness and salvation that instant, but she suddenly found herself back on her feet and able to enter her home safely. She later discovered that she was without a single bruise. Now Mrs P, in Christ, began to share her testimony with others, especially her peers.

Today, she is –

With Christ: It was just a few years after her conversion experience that Mrs P went to be with her Lord. It gave me and her family great peace of mind to know that she was now in the presence of Christ Jesus which, as another Paul stated, 'was far better'. To God be the glory.

9.

Mountains and Valleys

Volleyball players on a mountain, bathed in glorious sunshine, shoppers in the valley soaked with rain. Place – Kilchzimmer, 3,000 feet up in the Swiss Jura Mountains. Volleyball and shopping following lessons and chores at the Child Evangelism Fellowship Leadership Training Institute, August 1982. I was playing volleyball, Anne was shopping.

I was reminded of this scenario recently when I read somewhere that GEOGRAPHICALLY IT IS IMPOSSIBLE TO HAVE MOUNTAINS WITHOUT HAVING VALLEYS, I thought to myself that this is not only true in the GEOGRAPHICAL, but also true in the PHYSICAL, EMOTIONAL, MENTAL and SPIRITUAL. Everyone, Christian or otherwise will experience MOUNTAINS and VALLEYS in their lives. The contrast can be both amazing and overwhelming.

On another mountain top, this time a biblical one, we can only imagine the feelings of **awe**, **wonder** and **joy** which Peter,

Mountains and Valleys

James and John experienced on that mountain top usually entitled 'The Mount of Transfiguration'. Their Master, Jesus, resplendent in all his heavenly glory speaking with Moses and Elijah and the voice of God the Father, 'This is my beloved Son, listen to Him'. (Mark 9:7 NASB). Wow! Wouldn't you just loved to have been there?

But for every mountain top there is a deep, sometimes dark, valley. And so it was in our Bible episode; down in the valley things were different. There no joy was found only despair and disappointment and a sarcastic delight.

DESPAIR – A father had brought his son for healing. He went expectantly to the disciples but they were unable to help him.

DISAPPOINTMENT, even DISCOURAGEMENT – Jesus' disciples found they were powerless to help or heal the boy.

DELIGHT – The scribes and Pharisees in the crowd saw what they had longed for and now found.

Then Jesus comes down into the valley and suddenly everything changes. He heals the boy, changing the fathers despair to joy. His counsel restoring the faith of the disciples and the display of his miraculous power quelling the delight of the mockers. And He still displays his miraculous power today.

So, readers, are there valleys in your own lives? – Whatever they may be, remember, Jesus may not keep you out of the valleys, but he will certainly be there with you in your valleys. He will bring you to the MOUNTAIN TOP. He will dispel

Mountains and Valleys

your fears, help you to overcome your failures and, if needed, restore your faith.

ps. Jesus can turn all your valleys into – 'VALLEYS of SERVICE.

10.

Reflections

For those younger folk reading this, 1954 may seem like a thousand years ago. But for others, they might remember Gordon MacRae singing 'By the Light of the Silvery Moon'.

Now I have to smile when I think of the number of love songs which extol the beauty of the silver moon. But you know perhaps Pink Floyd were more accurate with their 'Dark Side of the Moon' because the moon is a dark planet. Hold on there, what about the bright moon we see in the night sky? Ah! It's all about reflection. That lovely silver moon is simply a reflection of our glorious sun.

I read recently about the town of Rjukan, Norway which because of its location among sheer mountains and of course it's northern latitude, does not see natural sunlight between the months of October and March. To overcome this the citizens installed large rotating mirrors on the mountainside

Reflections

to reflect the sun rays and beam welcome sunlight into the town square.

How are your reflecting qualities? Nothing to do with sunlight or moonlight but Christlikeness.

Jesus told his disciples, 'You are the light of the world' (Matthew 5:14) Is this not still a call to those of us who know Jesus as our Saviour, to reflect his love and grace and mercy and peace, whilst living in a world full of hatred and suffering and violence?

In his letter to the church at Ephesus, Paul writes (and this also applies to you and me), 'For you were once darkness, but now you are the light of life' (Ephesians 5:8).

So whatever the circumstances, and I know some of you may be in a dark place today, open your lives to the wonderful light of Jesus. He will cause his light to shine brightly into your situation, Jesus said, 'I am the light of the world. Whoever follows me will never walk in darkness, but have the light of life.' (John 8:12). Shine for him today and every day.

11.

Encouragement 1

Beside the Brook

How wonderful to read of our Sovereign God encouraging His children in distress. I'm thinking again about Elijah. Having delivered his message of judgement to King Ahab, Elijah finds himself subject to the subsequent drought and famine. (1st Kings 17)

But God! How often do we read these words in Scripture, 'but God'? – Our God responds so positively to obedience as we read how he encouraged Elijah by sustaining him with food brought by God-ordered ravens. Our wonderful God of the miraculous still sustains today those who trust in him.

'And my God shall supply all your needs. . .' (Philippians 4:19 NKJV).

Encouragement 1

I remember with a smile that once during our CEF® Isle of Man ministry we were back in Londonderry and Anne was sharing with a particular ladies group how God had supplied all our needs. We hadn't been there for a few years so one lovely wee lady, noticing Anne had put on some weight, remarked jokingly,

'I think he has supplied more than all your needs.'

But, seriously though, he does. Paul writes,

'Now to Him who is able to do immeasurably more than all we can imagine . . .' (Ephesians 3:2)

12.

Encouragement 2

Beside the 'Drying' Brook

The drought is severe, the brook is running dry, the ravens have gone. But, God is in control and has a new command for Elijah:

'Arise, Go to Zarephath, . . .'(1 Kings 17:9a NKJV)

Now, I wouldn't have been surprised if Elijah had exclaimed, 'Lord, you must be joking!'

Zarephath was located in dangerous territory – Jezebel's home territory. The land of the Baal god worshippers.

There was no such negative thinking from Elijah.

Elijah was trusting in his God!

Encouragement 2

Someone once said or wrote:

'The will of God will never take you, where the grace of God will not keep you!'

Remember and claim this for yourself. Perhaps at present you are in a spiritual wilderness. Grab hold of that portion of scripture, penned, we believe, by Jeremiah, 'his compassions fail not. They are new every morning: great is Thy faithfulness' (Lamentations 3:22b, 23 AV)

This scripture was used by God, many years ago, to rescue me from a spiritual drought.

Meanwhile, in your circumstances, whatever they may be, think on, and be obedient to, our miraculous, rescuing God.

I close with a verse that has been my guiding light through many difficult circumstances,

'Trust in the Lord with all your heart and lean not on your own understanding.' (Proverbs 3:5 NKJV)

13.

Encouragement 3

Beside the Dwindling Barrel

Imagine having to walk more than 170 kilometres during a period of drought, and through enemy territory. – That's what God told Elijah to do and thanks to King Ahab, Elijah had a price on his head.

'Go at once to Zarephath in the region of Sidon and stay there. I have directed a widow there to supply you with food.' (1 Kings 17:9)

Elijah arrived safely to Zarephath and entered by the town gate. – No one is recorded as having challenged him. – Why? Because he was trusting and obeying his God and that's where he saw the widow God had told him about. – Now comes Elijah's request and the widow's obedience.

Encouragement 3

'When he came to the town gate, a widow was there gathering sticks. He called to her and asked, 'Would you bring me a little water in a jar so I may have a drink?' As she was going to get it, he called, 'And bring me, please, a piece of bread.' (1 Kings 17:11,12)

She recognised Elijah for what he was, a man of God. Her reply:

'As surely as the LORD your God lives,' she replied, 'I don't have any bread, only a handful of flour in a jar and a little olive oil in a jug. I am gathering a few sticks to take home and make a meal for myself and my son, that we may eat it, and die.' (1 Kings 17:12)

Next we have obedience followed by a miracle.

'Elijah said to her, 'Don't be afraid. Go home and do as you have said. But first make a small loaf of bread for me from what you have and bring it to me, and then make something for yourself and your son. For this is what the LORD, the God of Israel, says: 'The jar of flour will not be used up and the jug of oil will not run dry until the day the LORD sends rain on the land.' She went away and did as Elijah had told her. So there was food every day for Elijah and for the woman and her family. For the jar of flour was not used up and the jug of oil did not run dry, in keeping with the word of the LORD spoken by Elijah.' (1 Kings 17:13 – 16)

What trust, in God, shown by both of our characters in this Bible passage! And reader, I have news for you, but some of

Encouragement 3

you know this already. – Elijah's God is still on the throne. – So we keep relying on God's word in all of our circumstances.

As Paul writes in his letter to the Philippians 'And **my God** will meet all your needs according to the riches of his glory in Christ Jesus.' (Philippians 4:19)

14.

Encouragement 4

Beside the Dying Boy

With God providing daily for all her needs, it would have been easy for the widow of Zarephath to think that at last all her troubles were over. But what a difference between verses 16 and 17 of 1 Kings chapter17.

'¹⁶ For the jar of flour was not used up and the jug of oil did not run dry, in keeping with the word of the LORD spoken by Elijah.

¹⁷ Sometime later the son of the woman who owned the house became ill. He grew worse and worse, and finally stopped breathing'

This widow was now a believer in the God of Elijah having experienced His power and provision. She was, just like Elijah, living by faith; faith in God. But, **faith is always tested.**

Encouragement 4

'For it has been granted to you on behalf of Christ not only to **believe** in him, but also to **suffer** for Him,' (Philippians 1:29)

Think of the psalmist, in the Old Testament. the New Testament apostles, the early believers and the Puritans in their day. Consider how much testing God's people on every hand are experiencing today; perhaps this applies even to you?

The record of God's loving dealings with two of His people who lived at Zarephath, which, significantly, means a place of refining, is highlighted in this biblical account.

Readers, if you are believers, men and women and young people of faith, you, and me, are living at Zarephath; in other words, we must expect our faith to be tested.

In v18 of 1 Kings 17 the scene changes. When the widow's son dies she behaves in an all too human fashion; she apportions blame. She turns on Elijah, and for a while her faith has temporarily collapsed. Interestingly though, when her faith was tested she remembered her sin: [18] She said to Elijah, 'What do you have against me, man of God? Did you come to remind me of my sin and kill my son?'

Notice:

This testing happened **suddenly.** It was unexpected, this illness and death. But, tests and trials can come, just like this, to God's people and we are not always forewarned and cannot always be forearmed.

This testing was **severe.** Not only did the child become ill, he died! And remember, this woman was already a widow!

When our first little girl was born, she was lovely. Anne, my wife, named her Avril, and she had dark hair and my dimple. The doctor thought she might have a heart problem so tests were carried out. Suddenly, unexpectedly, she died! Our hearts

Encouragement 4

were broken. Our two boys were devastated. But, God used this tragedy in the years to come.

This testing became a **service** to the glory of God.

In Zarephath, we see the fruit of Elijah's faith. First he prays, then he acts. Again he prays, and the child is restored to life. Now, Elijah hands him back to his mother. And the mother's faith is restored. (1 Kings 17:19–24).

In the case of our testing, after Anne went back to her job as a midwife, she came across other mothers who needed comforting. Just as the God of all comfort had comforted her in her loss, she was able to provide comfort to those grieving mothers. And, by God's comfort to us, our faith, just like that of the widow of Zarephath, is strengthened.

15.

Encouragement 5

**'The LORD—he is God! The LORD—
he is God!' (1 Kings 18:39b.)**

Our God is the God of the impossible. To prove this, climb with me to the top of Mount Carmel and witness an amazing miracle.

The people of Israel were torn apart between two gods; the gods of King Ahab and Queen Jezebel, and the God of Elijah. So on Mount Carmel, Elijah is about to have them make a choice.

A Christian I read about had a dilemma. He was being head hunted by another firm. Joining this firm would mean promotion and an increase in salary. It would, however, mean leaving home and close family. He was working with his present team but his dilemma was interfering with his work.

Encouragement 5

He had to make a choice. (I didn't find out which direction he chose, sorry. I would love to think, however, that he turned down the promotion, stayed with his family and worked hard at building up his present team).

Choices are sometimes difficult. The people of Israel compromised between worshipping God and sacrificing and praying to other gods, hoping if one couldn't help them, the other(s) would. The secular term is 'hedging their bets'.

I'm sure as you read this you know what God's people should do. But, knowing and doing are two different things. We are not unlike the people of Elijah's day. – As Christians, do we not sometimes 'hedge our bets'? – We know we should tithe, but do we, faithfully? With so many demands on our finances we can quote, but not always trust the promise of Philippians 4:19, which assures that: *'**My God** will **meet all your needs** according to the riches of his glory in Christ Jesus.'*

We rejoice in our forgiveness but forget the part that says: 'As we forgive those who sin against us.' (Matthew 6:12 New Living Translation).

Remember, the Lord has given us **new life**. We are to serve God and God alone, according to his word. Christian, are you dithering today?

The amazing miracles on Mount Carmel, recorded in 1Kings 18:20–39, and the results thereof, brought about the slaying of the false prophets, and the encouraging of the nation of Israel. May our God be the Encourager we need, to say with Joshua: 'But as for me and my household, we will serve the Lord.' (Joshua 24:15b).

16.

Encouragement 6

Getting through dark times

'What are you doing here, Elijah?'

God's question is found in 1 Kings 19:9 to the cowering, frightened Elijah, who had recently stood up in the power of God to the evil King Ahab and Queen Jezebel. Having witnessed the overpowering of the prophets of the false gods, he saw his prayer for rain answered, *(1 Kings 18 v 40 – 46),* but now, the death threats from Queen Jezebel sent Elijah scurrying off to hide in a cave on Mount Horeb.

(1 Kings 19:1): 'Now Ahab told Jezebel everything Elijah had done and how he had killed all the prophets with the sword. ² So Jezebel sent a messenger to Elijah to say, 'May the gods deal with me, be it ever so severely, if by this time tomorrow I do not make your life like that of one of them.'

Encouragement 6

If ever a man needed **more** encouragement, it was Elijah. I say more encouragement because, as we have already seen, encouragement is BIG in the Elijah saga. – And no one can encourage better than our wonderful God.

Recently I divided my garage into workshop and office. The office part was enclosed and insulated, walls and ceiling.

When my grandson Jack saw the office for the first time his reaction was,

'Wow, Grandad, what a man cave!'

I admit before that I had not heard the term before, but have heard it several times since, though not all referring to my 'man cave'. – It appears that a good number of men – and ladies too – have a personal 'cave'. The worst kind of 'cave' though, is that place in which you hide away from the pressures of coping in tough situations.

So we now read of Elijah cowering in his cave. But the God who sees his need, is the One who will turn Elijah's life around. And God reminds us in his word that he is 'the same yesterday and today and forever' (Hebrews 13:8), and 'Never will I leave you; never will I forsake you.'. (Hebrews 13:5).
Hiding in the dark will not make your problems disappear, indeed, like mushrooms, they tend to grow in the dark. God knows you are there. Speaking of the all-seeing, all-knowing God, the psalmist writes:

'Even the darkness will not be dark to you; the night will shine like the day, for darkness is as light to you.' (Psalm 139:12)

Encouragement 6

Turning lives around is part of God's plan as he sees and knows our circumstances and needs.

Encouragement is a big part of the ministry in which Anne and I are involved in our 'retirement.' – So, as we pray for you, our readers, we would ask that you pray for us.

17.

Spiritual Health

Having had heart problems and now currently fitted with a defibrillator, I am now on an exercise program to improve my cardiovascular fitness. This is so very important as several things happen physiologically in my body. The cardiovascular system – the oxygen transport system – has to get used to carrying oxygen in the blood through the blood vessels and deliver it as fuel for the muscles. Once the blood and oxygen arrives at the cellular level, the membranes of the cells must become 'trained' to allow the oxygen in so it can be used by the muscles. So the more I exercise, the more efficient this oxygen transport system becomes and my cardiovascular fitness improves. And of course this doesn't just apply to me; reader take note!

However, moving on from the physical to the spiritual, in a similar way, as we exercise aspects of our faith, we improve

Spiritual Health

our level of spiritual fitness. I can't remember where I read this but I felt it was worth passing on:

Our beliefs shape our attitudes, which shape our thinking patterns, which shape our behaviours. As we read the Bible our beliefs begin to align with the truths we read. If we're serious about growing in our faith, we'll be intentional about meditating on these biblical truths. Our repeated thoughts will grow our neural pathways. These repeated thoughts become our attitudes which will permeate our mind and our emotions, and end up shaping our will and its corresponding choices. This will determine our behaviours.

When my wife Anne saw me just after my operation, she remarked, 'Oh how well you look! I have found myself a new man!' I really am delighted about how I feel physically and want to continue in this vein. But when I read about what it means to be 'in Christ,' and for Christ to be 'in me.' I also rejoice and want to improve my spiritual wellbeing.

The Apostle Paul wrote: 'I have been crucified with Christ and I no longer live, but Christ lives in me. The life I now live in the body, I live by faith in the Son of God, who loved me and gave himself for me' (Galatians 2:20). This is true for each of us who have genuinely accepted Jesus as our Saviour. We are branches of a grapevine connected to its vine, who is Jesus, the Son of God. That's what the Word of God tells me:

'I am the vine; you are the branches. If you remain in me and I in you, you will bear much fruit; apart from me you can do nothing.' (John 15:5)

Spiritual Health

This is a supernatural, or spiritual, truth, and I believe it. The more I dwell on this truth, the more my attitude aligns with this truth. This enables me to 'rest' in my union with Jesus.
My life, – our lives, – should daily bear the fruit that Jesus' life is having through me, through us.

So let's get stuck in to our spiritual training. The more we dwell on the wonderful truths of God's Word and believe them, and trust that God's Son is living in and through us, our lives are changed. This is what Paul meant when he wrote:

'Therefore, if anyone is in Christ, *he is a new creation*; the old has gone, the new has come!' (2 Corinthians 5:15).

In Christ, I am a new creation! Just as our aerobic fitness level improves with regular exercise, our spiritual fitness matures when we embrace and practice God's truths.
So let our spiritual training commence and have a very blessed future, in Christ! Hallelujah!

18.

You are God's child

I remember reading – with great emotion – as Corrie ten Boom described her and her sister Betsie's horrific time in a Nazi concentration camp in the early 1940s. On one occasion, they were forced to take off their clothes during an inspection. Corrie stood in line feeling defiled and forsaken. Suddenly, she remembered that Jesus had hung naked on the cross. Struck with wonder and worship, Corrie whispered to her sister, 'Betsie, they took His clothes too.' Betsie gasped and said, Oh, Corrie, . . . and I never thanked Him.

Corrie's sister Betsy died in the notorious Ravensbrück concentration camp in 1944 but with a smile on her lips.

Before she died, she told Corrie, 'There is no pit so deep that he [God] is not deeper still.' We live in a world full of problems and struggles therefore, we need to remember what Jesus said: 'In this world you will have trouble. But take heart! I have overcome the world.' (John 16:32,33)

You are God's child

In Psalm 100:3 we are exhorted to: 'Know that the LORD is God. It is he who made us, and we are his; we are his people, the sheep of his pasture. Enter his gates with thanksgiving and his courts with praise; give thanks to him and praise his name.'

We live in a world of turmoil and tragedy but, as you remember who you are, you can respond in thanksgiving. For even in the worst of times, you can remember Christ's love and sacrifice. Don't let the brutality of the world take away your thankful heart. Remember **you are God's child**, and he has shown you his goodness and mercy through His work on the cross.

19.

Dealing with Doubt

This little portion from the 'helps' in my New King James Bible is something I would like to share.

'The cure for doubt depends on the thing doubted. However, the real problem is not in the object doubted, but in the subject who doubts.'

Therefore, the following steps in 'the cure for doubt' should be taken by the doubting **Christian.**

a. <u>Confess the doubt to God as sin.</u> Doubt is basically unbelief in God and His word and is therefore sin. 'But he who doubts is condemned. . . for whatever is not from faith is sin' (Romans 14:23 NKJV.) (although this scripture is about eating, the principle is the same)

In Hebrews 11:6 we read: 'But without faith it is impossible to please Him, (God)'*(NKJV)*

Dealing with Doubt

b. <u>Faithfully study the word of God.</u> 'Faith comes by hearing, and hearing by the word of God' (Romans 10:17 NKJV)

Through study and application of the Bible, our faith is strengthened and matured.

c. <u>Pray.</u> The surest way to face doubts when they come is to have an extensive past history of answered prayer. I believe that the more a Christian prays with faith, the more that Christian sees God answer prayer; the more a person sees God answer prayer, the stronger that person's faith becomes while the doubt becomes less.

Dealing with apparently unanswered prayer can also cause the Christian to doubt, so I include this wonderful piece by Bill Hybels:

- **<u>'No,' 'Slow,' 'Grow,' or 'Let's go!'</u>**

In his devotional book on 'How to cope with unanswered prayer,' Bill uses the above as God's answers. He suggests reading Isaiah 55 and Matthew: 9–13.

This is what he shares:

Introduction
- I've counselled countless people on the mystery and agony of unanswered prayer.

If the request is wrong, God will say, "No."
- Like us, the disciples made inappropriate requests of Jesus, and he said, "No."
- *Illustration: In this lengthy illustration, Hybels describes a time when the board of elders at his church prayed fervently*

for a person to fill a staff position. Once they had decided who they wanted to join the team, Bill sat down to lunch with the man and prayed that God would provide the right opportunity for him to make the offer. He sensed God saying, "No." Later, the elders discovered that the man had deception in his life and he would have been a bad fit for the job.

If the timing is wrong, God will say, "Slow."
- Like children, we dislike the words, "Not yet," as God shakes his head at us.
- God has reasons for his "Not yets;" we must not insist we know better than he.

If *you* are wrong, God will say, "Grow."
- Relational discord will cut us off from close fellowship with God.
- When we disobey, God says, "Why should I honour your requests when you don't honour mine?"

When the timing is right, God will say, "Let's go!"
- God *wants* to move that mountain for us; to change that circumstance; to answer that prayer.
- You'll be amazed at how often God will say, "Let's go!"

Conclusion
- I encourage you to follow the greatest pattern of prayer of all time: The Lord's Prayer. (used with permission)

(I found this extremely helpful. – I trust you will too.)

20.

Marching On!

We may never march with infantry – We're marching to Zion – Oh when the saints go marching . . . and so on. Great songs for, or about, marching. – Songs we have often sung.

Here in Northern Ireland we have what is called 'the marching season'. The main day is the 12th of July and many, including the saints, will go marching on.

For the Unionist Community the 12th of July is usually a day of picnics, parties, and parades. Other communities too have their days of marches and celebration, but there is no marching in unity or putting aside partisan differences and political perspectives.

Putting aside, however, what the marching season here in Northern Ireland is about and turning to God's Word, I find it interesting to note that the Apostle Paul actually uses the picture of a parade to teach the Corinthian believers an important biblical truth about the work of Jesus on our behalf.

Marching On!

In the second chapter of 2 Corinthians 14 (NKJV), he writes that God: 'always leads us in triumph in Christ' or in the New English Translation bible, – 'always leads us in triumphal procession, in Christ.'.

The Corinthians would have been very familiar with the idea of "triumphal processions." In fact, anyone living under the Roman Empire would have instantly pictured what Paul was describing.

(Historians tell us that whenever Roman forces captured another region, the victorious Roman commanding general would stage a parade. Gathering his victorious soldiers, he would march through the streets of the city with crowds lining the roads. The captured general and his subdued men would be forced to march, shackled and humbled, with the Roman forces to demonstrate the power and might of Rome's reach. While they marched, the pagan priests of Rome would burn incense to symbolize the sweet smell of victory.)

Paul now uses this scenario to illustrate the immensity of Christ's victory over sin and death in the lives of His followers. He reminds us as believers that spiritually we are being led in triumph by the all-conquering Jesus Christ and in a parade that displays his victory over the forces of evil. – But we are also reminded as Christians that we have been set free from our enslavement to sin, and, as we read in Paul's letter to the Romans, we are now; 'slaves to righteousness' (Romans 6:18). We have a new Master now that we have been gloriously set free!

Paul, with reference to the incense burned in the Roman procession, also reminds us that 'God . . . through us spreads everywhere the fragrance of the knowledge of Him' (2 Corinthians 2:14 English Standard Version). So, we are to be a sweet-smelling reminder of how attractive and appealing the freedom and victory we find in Jesus can be!

Today, and in the future, enjoy the parades. But if you are first and foremost a follower of Jesus, revel in the independence and freedom that you have found in him. Picture yourself being led through the streets of your towns and cities, on display to your friends and family as a trophy of Christ's victory. And pray that your encounters with others will leave behind the sweet smell of God's goodness. There will always be a hint (or perhaps more than a hint) of triumphalism but let it be seasoned with grace.

21.

The New Life

In a former ministry, Anne, my wife, and I used to sing in choirs, church meetings and gospel halls. Included in our repertoire was a frequently requested song, 'New Life in Christ (Abundant and Free).' – I believe that this new life can only be obtained 'by grace alone, through faith alone, in Christ alone.'

It is one thing to be convinced of the need for the new life, but it is an entirely different thing to acquire the new life. This new life means turning your back on the past. You are no longer the person you used to be. – In 2 Corinthians 5:17, it says that the new life believer is 'a new creation'; God 'has rescued us from the dominion of darkness and brought us into the kingdom of the Son he loves,' (Colossians 1:13); We are 'born again' (John 3:3 NKJV). And we have been adopted into God's family: – 'so that he could adopt us as his very own children.' (Galatians 4:5 New Living Translation)

The New Life

One of the most thrilling benefits of finding new life in Christ is that it is 'everlasting (eternal) life.'

To receive this new life means one enters into a new, personal relationship with God, a fullness of spiritual vitality, and this new life will *never die*. Anne and I have it; do you?

22.

Victorious Living (1)

The new life needs to become the victorious life. There are, however, somethings that prove a threat to living the victorious life. The Christian may be aware of them but find difficulty overcoming them.

I want to deal first with the problem of SIN.

a. <u>Sin is Significant</u>:

From my Sunday school days, I remember the definition from the shorter catechism (Westminster Confession of Faith).

'Sin is any want of conformity unto, or transgression of, the law of God.' Simply put, sin is disobeying God.

As David writes in Psalm 51:3&4:

Victorious Living (1)

'For I know my transgressions, and my sin is always before me'. 'Against you, you only, have I sinned and done what is evil in your sight;'

b. Sin is Serious:

'But your iniquities have separated you from your God; your sins have hidden his face from you, so that he will not hear.' (Isaiah 59:2). – Of all people, David had good reason for feeling guilty. – Most commentators believe that David wrote Psalm 32 after he cried out to God for forgiveness. David's confession was for a double sin, adultery and murder. (More about this in the following devotional.)

c. Sin is Suppressing:

It can suppress our conscience sometimes to the extent we bury our sin in a sea of forgetfulness. This happened to David and it took a story from the Prophet Nathan to stir him to repentance. You can read about this in 2 Samuel 12:4–9.

We read in Psalm 38 that David's guilt was obviously immense!

He writes, 'My guilt has overwhelmed me like a burden too heavy to bear.' (Psalm 38:4)

If this applied to David, it applies to you and to me. Thank God for the assurance that:

'If we confess our sins, He is faithful and just and will forgive us our sins and cleanse us from all unrighteousness.' (1 John 1:9 NKJV)

David's release was sweet: 'Blessed is the one whose transgressions are forgiven, whose sins are covered.' (Psalm 32:1)

Victorious Living (1)

Perhaps you need this blessed sweetness today. If so, confess your sin, repent of your sin (that means a total turning away, never going back): – receive that blessed assurance of forgiveness and assurance. Walk with God in victorious living.

23.

Victorious Living (2)

Temptation is a major problem the Christian must cope with. Praise God, you are never alone in dealing with temptation, as Paul reminds each of us:

'No **temptation** has overtaken you except what is common to mankind. And God is faithful; he will not let you be tempted beyond what you can bear. But when you are tempted, he will also provide a way out so that you can endure it' (1 Corinthians 10:13)

Reader, if you are not a Christian, don't think Satan will pass you by. Satan hates all God's creatures especially mankind, so temptation, his key weapon, is apportioned to the saint and sinner alike. The saint however can claim the above verse with confidence. The saint is not as is supposed, a person with a halo who has been canonised because of exception holy living. No, Paul describes a saint as one who has trusted in, and is living for, Jesus Christ. e.g. in Ep*hesians* 1:1 (NASB)

Victorious Living (2)

'Paul, an apostle of Christ Jesus by the will of God, To the saints who are in Ephesus, and are faithful in Christ Jesus:'
Look how some in Scripture behaved when tempted:

a. David, we mentioned him in Devotional 19.
Instead of being with his army, we find him on his roof; watching a lady bathing. – The lady was Bathsheba, and David was filled with lust. – So, what did he do? He **looked**, he **lingered** and then, he **lost** his battle with temptation. – He committed adultery, and then conspired with his general to have Bathsheba's soldier husband Uriah, murdered.
(2 Samuel 2).

b. Joseph: sold into slavery but he found favour with his master, Potiphar. – He also found favour with his master's wife who lusted after him. – Although having many opportunities presented to him, Joseph refused to commit adultery with her. (Genesis 39)

c. Jesus: tempted by Satan while he was physically weak in the wilderness. How did Jesus respond to Satan's temptations? He responded with the word of God, and Satan was soundly defeated. (Matthew 4)

How should you and I respond to Satan's tempting?
1. **Immediately** (don't be a David.)
2. **Consistently** (follow Joseph's example)
3. **Ruthlessly** (just as Jesus did,) using 'the sword of the Spirit, which is the word of God'. (Ephesians 6:17b NKJV).

24.

Blessed Assurance

There is nothing like a not too hot bath with a, 'stress-relieving additive' in the water, especially after a time working in the garden. Such a bath does ease the aches and pains, but from experience, and at my age, the relief is usually short-lived. I mention all of the above, not to gain your sympathy, but to use it as an illustration of a spiritual problem, or problems, that some Christians can experience: –

The past. – I've written about past problems before, but I make no apologies for mentioning it again. – Christian, Satan hates you, and will do all in his power to bring you down. Perhaps someone reading this is not what is termed a 'born again believer'. Well I have new for you. – Satan hates you too! – Even though you may not be a Christian in the biblical sense, you have been created in the image of God and GOD LOVES YOU and he, Satan, rejoices over your spiritual condition.
For the Christian though, Satan has a special hatred and desire. That desire is to cause you (a) to doubt your salvation and

Blessed Assurance

(b) to doubt your worthiness. – This brings about a lack of assurance as to your standing before God. But, perhaps like my soak in the bath this morning which temporarily alleviated my physical problems, you need something like a really good spiritual soak. – No, I'm not talking about baptism by immersion, I will leave that to the subscribing denominations.

So, how does the Christian solve these spiritual problems? The Christian must learn to **soak** in **Christ**! – Christ is the answer to all our spiritual sores and dilemmas. – So what do I do when at times I might feel a bit spiritually low? – I read Paul's letter to the Colossians. – I read it again and again. – It helps me to soak in Christ and this soothes and heals. – But, you need permanent immersion and daily cleansing.

Remember, 'the blood of Jesus (God's) Son purifies us from **ALL SIN'.** (1 John 1:7), past and present. And it is ongoing! **'If we confess** our sins, he is faithful and just and will forgive us our sins and purify us from all unrighteousness.' (1 John 1:9) – Trusting everything to Jesus Christ and His word will bring **blessed assurance.**

25.

Will You Go?

When my eldest sons were growing up in Christian music, they introduced me to Stewart and Kyle. – I have used their lyrics in various sermons down through the years, and one lyric in particular, because it made a big impression on me. – The lyric has a fictional conversation between God the Father and God the Son, but in my imagination I can almost hear that conversation taking place.

'Jesus, I want you to go to earth and give your life for the sinner.' – Is the first line of the lyric, which goes on to ask Jesus: *'Will you go?'*

Then in the lyric Jesus answers, *'Yes Father, I will go. My life is yours to use. I will tell the world that you alone are God of all.'*

As the conversation continues, the Father tells the Son what he will suffer, physically, emotionally and spiritually.

Will You Go?

The final stanza of the song reminds us that:

'He came, and he died on a cross, just for you and you're looking at his love, perfect love.'

The lyric echoes the *wonderful message of 1 Corinthians 15:3,4* '[3]For what I received I passed on to you as of first importance that Christ died for our sins according to the Scriptures, [4] that he was buried, that he was raised on the third day according to the Scriptures.'

I searched for the Stewart and Kyle 'Yours Ever' for a number of years without success. – I could only find their CD in a German online shop but money exchange proved difficult. Just last year I found a new CD in iTunes, 'The best of Stewart and Kyle,' iTunes now have their CD's to download. May I highly recommend them to you.

I assure you I am not an agent for Stewart and Kyle but I have found their lyrics both inspirational and prophetic.

26.

Ransomed *healed, restored, forgiven*

> **Praise, my soul, the King of heaven,**
> **To his feet thy tribute bring;**
> **Ransomed, healed, restored, forgiven,**
> **Who like me his praise should sing?**
> **Alleluia! Alleluia!**
> **Praise the everlasting King.**
> (Henry Francis Lyte)

All of us, I'm sure, know what it means to be kidnapped; hopefully none have experienced the trauma. – But, most, maybe all, have read about it or watched it happen in film or TV.

Someone is taken and a ransom demanded, usually a sum of money. While we may never have been kidnapped, we have been ransomed. In biblical times a slave could, for a sum of money, be set free.

Ransomed *healed, restored, forgiven*

An amazing ransom has been paid to set men, women, boys and girls free from the worst kind of slavery; the slavery of sin. Jesus gave His life to set us free from the slavery of sin. As the song by John Moore song says:

> *'All my iniquities on him were laid,*
> *He nailed them all to the tree.*
> *Jesus, the debt of my sin fully paid,*
>   *He paid the ransom for me.*

The 2006 film *'Amazing Grace'* told the story about the campaign against the slave trade led by William Wilberforce, who was responsible for steering anti-slave trade legislation through Parliament. – The film also recounts the experiences of John Newton as a crewman on a slave ship and his subsequent conversion to Christ. – Liberated from the slavery of sin by Christ Jesus he later wrote the poem which was put to music and which we still sing today – 'Amazing Grace.'

But moving from the wonderful freedom found in Christ to another desperate need for freedom; a freedom from modern-day slavery. I believe that all of us for whom Christ paid that supreme ransom should be aware that across the globe, an estimated 35.8 million people are currently living in modern-day slavery. Stripped of their dignity and humanity; forced to work effectively without pay; trapped behind bars and worse, the world's most vulnerable sentenced to a lifetime of rape, abuse and extreme labour.

Spiritual slavery; release from the bonds of sin and human slavery; release from the profiteers.

Brothers and sisters in Christ, for both situations: – Let us pray!

27.

ransomed Healed *restored, forgiven*

Close to completing our course, at the Leadership Training Institute now called the Children's Ministry Leadership Course (CMLC)® at Kilchzimmer, Switzerland, in 1989, Anne had the unfortunate experience of falling downstairs and tearing ligaments in her left leg. – On advice, she declined an operation in Switzerland, so she attended graduation wearing a knee-length plaster of Paris. Back home, having been interviewed and accepted by the CEF (Child Evangelism Fellowship®) National Committee, we prepared for ministry as local directors in our home area of north-west Ulster. The Commissioning Service was to be held in our local church, Ebrington Presbyterian. – Anne was determined she was not going to the front wearing a plaster so, at the local hospital, she prayed fervently for healing. – The plaster was removed, her leg was X-rayed, and no ligament damage was found, not even scar tissue, even though Anne had the Swiss X-rays with her which showed ligament damage. Anne walked down the

ransomed Healed *restored, forgiven*

church aisle plaster-free. 'I am the God that healeth thee' (Exodus 15:26 AV).

Fast forward to the Isle of Man 1992. – Things were not going well with me health-wise; arthritis was causing me lots of left hand and arm pain. – Guitar playing was becoming difficult, as was driving. – Travelling to take an assembly one morning, I was listening to a tape of an American Christian artist, Don Meon, singing a song based on Exodus 15:26 (AV), 'I am the God that healeth thee.' Don then spoke and said:

'Do you believe this?'

As I travelled I prayed, with my eyes open of course.

'Yes Lord, I believe. Help my unbelief.'

The sensation that travelled through my body was indescribable, and right there and then the pain in my left hand and arm was gone. – Now in my older years, I still have problems with arthritis, but I have never again experienced the arthritic pain I had during that period in the Isle of Man. Without that healing, my ministry would have suffered and the *work which followed* would have been extremely difficult. There is an even more important healing though, the healing of the soul. This comes about when lives that are scarred by sin find healing when committed and surrendered to Christ.

> 'He was wounded for our transgressions,
>
> He was bruised for our iniquities;
>
> The chastisement for our peace was upon Him,
>
> And by His stripes we are healed.'
>
> Isaiah 53:5 (NKJV)

ransomed Healed *restored, forgiven*

Now to him who is able to do exceedingly abundantly above all that we ask or think, according to the power that works in us, to him *be* glory in the church by Christ Jesus to all generations, forever and ever. Amen.

Ephesians 3:20,21(NKJV)

28.

*r*ansomed, healed, *Restored, forgiven*

I'm sure there are times when many Christians feel spiritually low and God seems far away. Or perhaps reading this you know you have drifted away from your once close relationship with God. I remember a time when I was feeling cold spiritually, and I was finding difficulty even praying; the reasons I won't go into. I was staying with Anne's sister Muriel and her husband Billy, and they had insisted on giving me their bedroom. That night, I felt quite low; I just knelt, wordlessly, before the Lord. I slept well, and when I woke the following morning, I saw something I hadn't seen the night before. The curtains were open just a chink, and a ray of sunlight fell on a framed tapestry on the opposite wall. When I thought about that picture in later years, it seemed to be quite large, but when Muriel gave Anne and me that tapestry some years later, I discovered it was just nine inches long by four inches wide. So, why was this morning in Muriel and Billy's bedroom a life-changing experience? It was because of the words on this tapestry, a portion of scripture that, to this day, is precious to me. The words are found in the Book of Lamentations, in Chapter Three and verses twenty-two and twenty-three: '. . . his compassions fail not, they are new every morning: great is Thy faithfulness (AV).'

I realised that my God hadn't moved; I had. Now, with His great love for me, God was drawing me back. I have used this wonderful act of grace during the countless times I have given my testimony or a sermon. What a great and faithful God we, as Christians, have. Restoration, hurting or drifting Christian, is only a prayer away.

29.

ransomed, healed, restored, Forgiven

I've said it before and I say it again **Sin is serious!** We will never be without its presence until we go to glory.

I remember when teaching this subject at a children's meeting, I mentioned that sometimes I sin. A lad put up his hand and, interrupting me in my flow, said, 'But you're a minister, how can you sin?' This gave me a wonderful opportunity to remind him of the memory verse from the Bible that the class had learned earlier in our meeting. 'All have sinned, and fall short of the glory of God', sometimes in bad thoughts, sometimes by bad things we do and sometimes by the bad things we say.'

In Luke 7 verses 36–50 we read of the woman who anointed Jesus feet in the home of Simon the Pharisee. In these verses we read of Simon pointing out this woman's sins of commission. [39] When the Pharisee who had invited him saw this, he said to himself, 'If this man were a prophet, he would know who is touching him and what kind of woman she is – that she is a sinner.'

Later we read of Jesus pointing out to Simon his sins of omission. [44] Then he turned towards the woman and said to Simon, 'Do you see this woman? I came into your house. You did not give me any water for my feet, but she wet my feet with her tears and wiped them with her hair. [45] You did not give me a kiss, but this woman, from the time I entered, has not stopped kissing my feet. [46] You did not put oil on my head, but she has poured perfume on my feet.

Followed by the wonderful conclusion:

[47] Therefore, I tell you, her many sins have been forgiven – as her great love has shown. But whoever has been forgiven little loves little.'

[48] Then Jesus said to her, 'Your sins are forgiven.'

[49] The other guests began to say among themselves, 'Who is this who even forgives sins?'

[50] Jesus said to the woman, 'Your faith has saved you; go in peace.' (Luke Ch. 7)

Forgiveness, of course, works both ways. In his book 'The Forgotten F Word' Robin Oake the former Chief Constable in the Isle of Man and a former elder in Port St. Mary Baptist Church, tells the tragic story of the murder of his son Stephen. Stephen was a police officer killed in the line of duty. The

ransomed, healed, restored, Forgiven

press marvelled at how Robin was able to forgive his son's killer. But Robin was a man steeped in scripture and close to his saviour who knew that forgiveness was not an option but a command, and for Robin and his wife Christine, the only way forward. If the book is still in print it is well worth reading.

> **Ransomed, healed, restored, forgiven,**
> **Who like me his praise should sing?**

30.

Vedi, Veni, Veci

No! I haven't got my Latin words in the wrong order.

Probably you are more familiar with the words written to Rome by Caesar in 47 BC after his defeat of Pharnaces of Pontus. He wrote Veni (I came), Vedi (I saw), Vici (I conquered) but I was thinking of another conqueror whose amazing accomplishment turned the phrase around.

In the Old Testament we read how God saw the needs of his people in Egypt and sent Moses. But in the New Testament we read that God **saw** the need of the world and **came** in the person of His Son Jesus who, after living a sinless life during which He taught, preached and healed, Jesus carried out his final and most wonderful accomplishment when He allowed Himself to suffer and die on a cruel cross. On that cross He **conquered** sin turning away God's wrath against sinful man and bringing forgiveness to all who put their trust in Him. He

Vedi, Veni, Veci

conquered Satan who thought the death of Jesus was his victory only to discover it was his defeat. Jesus then **conquered** death when he rose from the grave and finally **conquered** time and space when He returned to the glory from whence He came.

One day He will return, as the angels told his watching disciples, 'This same Jesus, who has been taken from you into heaven, will come back in the same way as you have seen Him go into heaven' (Luke 1:11)

I close by quoting the words of Christopher Wordsworth from his 1862 hymn:

> Who is this that comes in glory,
> With the trump of jubilee?
> Lord of battles, God of armies,
> He has gained the victory.
> He who on the cross did suffer,
> He who from the grave arose,
> He has vanquished sin and Satan,
> He by death has spoiled His foes.

31a.

Nevertheless

'For the eyes of the LORD range throughout the earth to strengthen those whose hearts are fully committed to him.' (2Chronicles 16:9a)

Among my archives I came across this gem for Max Lucado from his book 'facing your giants'. I pass it on in the hope it will encourage you as it certainly encouraged me.

The king and his men marched to Jerusalem to attack the Jebusites, who lived there. The Jebusites said to David, 'You will not get in here; even the blind and the lame can ward you off.' They thought, 'David cannot get in here.' <u>Nevertheless,</u> David captured the fortress of Zion—which is the City of David.2 Sam. 5:6–7)

Did you see it? Most hurry past it. Let's not. *(that is why I have underlined it in bold. Max calls it a twelve letter-masterpiece.)*

Nevertheless

Wouldn't you like God to write a *nevertheless* in your biography? Born to alcoholics, *nevertheless* she led a sober life. Never went to college, *nevertheless* he mastered a trade. Didn't read the Bible until retirement age, *nevertheless* he came to a deep and abiding faith.

We all need a *nevertheless*. And God has plenty to go around. Strongholds mean nothing to him. Remember Paul's words? 'The weapons we fight with are not the weapons of the world. On the contrary, they have divine power to demolish strongholds.' 2 Cor. 10:4. (NIV)

You and I fight with toothpicks; God comes with battering rams and cannons. What He did for David, He can do for *you*. The question is, will *you* do what David did? The King models much here.

Two types of thoughts continually vie for your attention. One proclaims God's strength; the other lists your failures. One longs to build you up; the other to tear you down. And here's the great news: you select the voice you hear. Why listen to the mockers? Why heed their voices? Why give ear to pea-brains and scoffers when you can, with the same ear, listen to the voice of God?

Do what David did. Turn a deaf ear to the old voices. Open a wide eye to the new choices. Who knows, you may be a prayer away from a *nevertheless*. God loves to give them.

Peter stuck his foot in his mouth. Joseph was imprisoned in Egypt. The Samaritan woman had been married five times. Jesus was dead in the grave. . .

Nevertheless

Nevertheless, Peter preached, Joseph ruled, the woman shared, Jesus rose??? and you?

You fill in the blank. Your *nevertheless* awaits you.

Copyright (W Publishing Group, 2006) Max Lucado. (adapted by me to the glory of God)

31 b.

The Dream

Michael Perrot, an accomplished counsellor and speaker, was used by God in helping Anne and I to grow in our Christian faith. I was asked to sing at a meeting at which Michael was speaking (this was many years ago) and his message that evening had a profound effect on me. He spoke of Heaven, and the joy there when one sinner comes to repentance (Luke 15:10) and with a little license, imagined a sadness in heaven when one rejects Christ.

Later that night, at home, I began to put Michael's subject down as a poem, a poem that down through the years has been a form of encouragement to many Christians with regards to prayer and outreach.

So I have chosen to close this devotional booklet with my poem entitled 'The Dream'

The Dream

*I dreamed I walked the streets of heaven with the
Saviour by my side,*

*And He showed me lovely dwellings where the
saved in Christ abide.*

*I could hear their joyful singing, songs of
praises filled the air*

*And the peace of God was present, love was
smiling everywhere.*

*Then, suddenly, their songs were silent, as
before me dark and bare*

*Stood a house with windows shuttered,
'Who,' I thought, 'was living there?'*

*So I asked the Saviour with me, 'who could
own that lonely home?'*

*Then, with tear filled eyes he answered,
'twas for one who would not come.'*

*Sadness filled the streets of heaven as the
saviour gently cried,*

*'Go and tell them how I love them, they're
the reason why I died.'*

*Won't you hear the saviour's message?
Please don't turn your hearts away.*

*Jesus, from the streets of heaven, gently calls,
'Oh come, today!'*

Roy Porter 1964